S

LAURA DING-EDWARDS

STILL

The information given in this book should not be treated as a substitute for professional medical advice. Always consult a medical practitioner.

Although every effort has been made to ensure that the information in this book was correct at press time, no responsibility is assumed for any loss, damage, or disruption caused by errors or omissions and no liability is assumed for any damaged that may result from the use of this information.

The views expressed in this book are those of the author alone and do not necessary reflect those of That Guy's House.

This book is a work of nonfiction, however, certain elements may have been fictionalized to suit the narrative.

The book information is catalogued as follows;

Author Name(s): Laura Ding-Edwards

STILL

Description; First Edition

1st Edition, 2021

Book Design by Lynda Mangoro

Original artwork by Laura Ding-Edwards

ISBN (paperback) 978-1-914447-21-1

ISBN (ebook) 978-1-914447-22-8

Published by That Guy's House

www.ThatGuysHouse.com

STILL

For my magic, Dotty Raine

FOREWORD

Thanks for being here with me for my second book, the follow up to The Mountain.

I can't believe I am fortunate enough to be releasing a second collection of poetry and I hope you enjoy it, or at least that it evokes some emotion

This collection still has the usual themes of mental health, self love, the best and worst of human beings, but it also incorporates my new role of becoming a Mum and also a little of the craziness of the last year or two as a whole.

This year especially has been a huge eye opener for many of us and I'm sure we could all write a book about our experiences in 2020, so I hope that some of what I've captured relates to your feelings, or gives you an insight into how others have viewed it.

I hope you have the space and time to sit and absorb the words I've written & enjoy them as much as I've enjoyed creating them for you.

With love,

Laura

CONTENTS

PROSE

Poems

Laura Ding-Edwards

THE MIDDLE

You may not be the prettiest

You might not be the best

You don't have all the clothes and shoes

Or makeup like the rest

You might not win on sports day

Or ever get picked first

You're not the fastest runner

But you're also not the worst

You might not get the A stars

Or the headteacher's award

Sometimes you thrive in classrooms

Other days you're super bored

You're the middle ground, an in-between

You're neither first or last

Not party to the popular

Nor a singular outcast

You're schooldays aren't a living hell

You survive with means and ways

You wouldn't say they're awful

But they're not your best of days

Because those days are still to come

Not everyone will thrive

The academic mainstream

It's after this you'll come alive

You'll find the people just like you

The ones who don't quite fit

The confines of the playground

Still

And everything that comes with it
Til then believe me when I say
Your life is not just school
You'll flourish on the other side
And it won't matter if you're cool
It won't matter if you win each race
Or score the highest test
There's so much more to learn
The world will teach you this the best
So worry not if school's a drag
Muddle through as best you can
Get in, get out & do your best
And trust life's bigger plan

BE

Be humble in your wrongs because nobody's always right

Be soft in your approach because not all have your insight

Be cautious in your trust for all that glitters isn't gold

Be truthful in your stories as they often get retold

Be sparing with your secrets, some friends outlast loyalties

Protect your gentle heart, don't give all and sundry keys

Be generous with kindness, love the lost and lonely first

Be willing with forgiveness, let your bitterness disperse

Use your own two ears to listen and your own two eyes to see

Be faithful to yourself and keep your love & spirit free

LUNA

She shines like the moon
So soft and serene
Reflecting the light
Of the sun, unseen
With no ceremony
Or arrogance, pride
She moves every ocean
Each worldly tide
The Queen of the night
While the universe sleeps
She comforts and carries
And soothes, safely keeps
The secrets of midnight
The songs of the stars
The tears of the broken
A moment that's ours
No moonrise or moonset
No stifling heat
Just constantly present
With every heartbeat
She wraps up so gently
The depths of my soul
So that even in darkness
I know I am whole

F LY

Another persons fortune

Has no effect on yours

The world does not distribute good

Based on your perceived flaws

Picking holes in others

Does not determine wealth

A jealous, angry mindset

Is no good for your health

Hating on the winners

Won't make you a success

People who work hard for more

Aren't the reason you have less

Believing idle gossip

And spreading it with glee

Won't make you more popular

Don't be governed by envy

The more you tear down others

To fill the gaps inside

The more you'll feel the burning

That comes with that divide

There's space for everyone

To reach up for the stars

Stop measuring your worth

By theirs and yours and ours

Still

Pull each other closer

Hold each other high

Declare your kin as humankind

And help each other fly

WALK WITH ME

Walk with me in sunshine
When the world is in your side
When your heart is singing loudly
I will sing your song with pride

Walk with me in moonlight
When the world has fallen still
When you feel alone and empty
I will help your soul refill

Walk with me in thunder
Let your turmoil overflow
I will ride the lightening with you
Watch the world get lost below

Walk with me in heavy rain
The kind that lasts all day
Let hot tears roll like dice
Fall off your cheeks and wash away

Walk with me when times are tough
And walk when they are fine
Walk when you are at your best
And when you're out of line

Still

Walk with me beneath the stars
And up above them too
I'll walk this earthly path
Then walk in heaven beside you

CLOSE

Rough winds will blow

Days grey and slow

Just drizzle and damp and dark

Amongst the breeze

Wet, leafless trees

Sway lifeless, sad and stark

The minimal light,

forever night

Eternal off-white gloom

A distant haze

Of summer days

And life in it's full bloom

But do not fear

"I'm almost here"

Spring whispers in the air

"Look for the light,

The longest night

Has passed - we're nearly there"

The veil will lift,

A tangible shift

In scent and touch and song

The birds will speak

We've climbed the peak

New life will be along

Just hold your nerve,

Your strong reserve

For just a while more

Still

Not far from here

A distant cheer

That winter's closed the door

MAGICAL

What a magical pair of mammaries

And what wonderful wobbly bits!

What a beautiful, bumbly tummy

And a bottom that perfectly sits

Atop your fabulous thighs

And your spangly, sparkly calves

With your gorgeous, knobbly kneecaps

You really don't do things by half!

What frivolous, flirtatious freckles

On your splendid, snuffly nose

My Goodness, you really are special

From your head to the tips of your toes!

There's immeasurable beauty within you

I can feel it like sunshine in June

You radiate moonbeams and magic

Your existence lights up the room

Quick! Go and see for yourself now

Its time that your wings were uncurled

Stand tall and stand proud and say with me

"I can take on the rest of the world!"

FLOURISH

It's better to be an outsider
Than be inside and selling your soul
There's nothing that makes you more special
Than avoiding the perilous hole
Of blindly, begrudgingly following
The morbid, monotonous crowd
That don't take a second to process
The things that have made them too proud
To question the news and the papers
The rat race that has them encased
In the perfectly pointless existence
Of numbers without names or a face
Step out of the line and break silence
Believe you can do your own thing
Every person deserves time to flourish
And find out what makes their heart sing
Our time is so short and so precious
Don't waste it with boredom & hate
Burst open your true inner passion
And live fully, before it's too late.

Laura Ding-Edwards

TWO STEPS BEHIND

I used to walk two steps behind
Head down, safe in the shade
Not brave enough to break the line
A little girl, afraid

A face that fits, a voice that's heard
With these I wasn't blessed
And so I followed quietly
In the footsteps of the rest

They say that you can see it
The privileged elite
The ones who never tiptoed
Who only saw their own two feet

But something changed within me
And I felt the tidal pull
Of the warrior inside
And the strength of me in full

My song began so softly
Testing water, breaking ground
A step aside, minority
With nobody around

Still

And gradually, I found it
My brave, lioness heart
I wish I'd trusted sooner
The voice there from the start

And now I sing out proudly
Shout freely from the roof
I suppressed the song inside me
But now I speak my truth

WOUNDS

I know your wounds are not your fault

They never are you see

But you won't heal what hurt you

By inflicting them on me

I know the thought of someone else

In pain takes yours away

But honestly; it doesn't work

It's just a short delay

It feels better now

And maybe for a while after

But hear me when I say

You're only putting on a plaster

For all the time you carry on

Attacking those who love you

You're building up a wall

That's getting harder to break through

You can't be held responsible

For the pain that you've been dealt

But you are now accountable

For how others have felt

By your words and by your actions

From the wounds you're passing on

To the undeserving victims

Still

And the innocent anon

Break the vicious cycle

Be brave and face your pain

Stop passing on your anger

And return to peace again

I AM

I am small but I am strong

I am young yet I am wise

I am human, filled with magic

I am me but in disguise

I am kind but I am tough

I am weak in times of woe

I am sometimes moving forward

I am sometimes much too slow

I am all the stars, the universe

A feeling you can trust

I am oceans, I am sunlight

I am air, I rise from dust

I am fire, fuel and fauna

I am rooted to the Earth

I move with tides and moonscapes

I am death

I am rebirth

I am silence, I am darkness

I am bright and brilliant light

I am quiet winter mornings

I am summer swifts in flight

I am North and South

The East, the West

I'm all night parties

Days of rest

I'm all and nothing in between

Still

A mirror, window, wall
Everything is part of me
I am part of it all

Laura Ding-Edwards

FROM MINE

When all around is falling, failing
Fraying at the seams
When life feels like a nightmare
And you can't recall your dreams

When self-care is barely eating
And the days bleed into nights
When you can't remember compliments
Just bad mistakes and fights

When your body's treading water
And your soul is drowning fast
When you cannot focus on your wins
Just the times when you were last

When colours lose their vibrancy
And sunlight hurts your eyes
When you wish the world could stop
While you work out how to survive

Trust your breath and body
Forgive your broken mind
You deserve this time to heal
Don't blame yourself, be kind

Still

You are unique, worthy, wonderful
Your story is compelling
I know it's hard; believe me
It's a tale I'm used to telling

We humans are so fragile
But together we create
A formidable bond
Beneath our altered mental state

Trust the tide will turn again
One small step at a time
I'll wait here for you, darling
To your broken heart, from mine x

REBIRTH

The last of the leaves lose their grip
As the earth sinks, heavy and full
The daylight retreats, slowly fading
As all fauna prepares for its cull

Fields lie lit only by moonlight
Through ominous, heaving cloud
Furrows of navy and indigo
Tracks left by nights sombre shroud

The pavement holds mirrors to street lights
Wet ink on the years open book
Old stories of summer and sunshine
Seem frail; a dream we mistook

The crisp of midwinter moves closer
A cleaner, more clinical space
The traces of sodden December
The year hidden, without a trace

And the light will return, at first gently
A welcome, familiar face
Where snowdrops replace mulch & fungus
The bluebells return to their place

Still

The darkness releases its stronghold

Life, once again, finds a way

The circle of growth is unending

Each night always gifts a new day

CHRISTMAS

Not everyone loves Christmas

Although it might seem strange

Some people just don't like the fuss

And long to rearrange

The pressures of perfection

Sensory overload

Hearts that ache for absentees

Heads threatening to explode

The lonely and the lost ones

The penniless and poor

No presents, food or sparkling tree

No family at the door

So please don't think us rude

Ungrateful, self absorbed

It's just at times these big events

Are easier ignored

Enjoy the day you're given

Love and understand

That those who don't love Christmas

Might need a helping hand

WOMAN

Woman is the mountain
Constant, strong and solid
Through sisterhood and solitude
Paths easy and paths torrid

Woman is the turquoise lake
Quiet, calm and still
Reflection, peaceful interlude
To cure internal ill

Woman is the moon and stars
A guide in darkest night
Magic from the depths of time
Soothing, celestial light

Woman is the ocean tide
Blood and breath and birth
The link to ancient secrets
The spirit of the Earth

Woman is infinite skies
The ground beneath our feet
The fire, wind, the soil and rain
Both glory and defeat

Laura Ding-Edwards

Woman is all seasons

All elements and verse

Every part of time and space

Woman – know your worth

INSIDE

I've been many places
But the best of them all
Is a place deep inside me
Safe quiet and small

A tiny escape room
Barely used, empty space
Safe and secure
A moment of grace

Away from the chaos
A break for my mind
Where no-one can find me
And all words are kind

No self deprecation
Or insecure doubt
I whisper and wonder
No need here to shout

We all need a moment
A rest from the norm
A harbour to anchor
And weather the storm

Laura Ding-Edwards

Be still for a minute
Hold onto the peace
Find your way quietly
To this place of release

It might take some practice
But I promise it's there
When you get there you'll know
Find your place & take care

HOLD ON

Just one more second

One more minute

It feels like hell

When you're deep in it

Count each step

Each moment passed

Know your mind

Is built to last

Each tick of time

Has been and gone

Take every one

As proof you're strong

A deep breath in

And on we go

And even if

It feels too slow

Know this, my friend

It slips away

Too soon a second

Becomes a day

Day gives to night

The weeks shall flow

Season by season

Less far to go

So hold on, please

We'll walk together

The path is long

Laura Ding-Edwards

But it's not forever

Just one more second

One more minute

For even hell

Has it's limit

TOMORROW

When things just haven't gone your way

And it feels bad luck is here to stay

When life feels like an uphill climb

And nothing seems to stay in line

When you're juggling the house and kids

You find the pots but not the lids

When work is tough, the weather's wet

You haven't done the dishes yet

The car is due it's MOT & cries of

"There's nothing on TV"

Fill your ears on wild repeat

Along with "there's nothing here to eat"

When Instagram is full of pics

Of perfect Mums with their blue ticks

Spotless kids with vegan brunch

While you forgot your eldest's lunch

Show homes grey & sparkling white

Take a look at your bomb site

And realise how much love is here

As the baby bites the old dog's ear

And little socks hang strewn around

Toys and felts left on the ground

Yes you're busy, yes you're stressed

Some days you're barely up and dressed

But what better reason to be tired

Than family by whom you're so admired

Laura Ding-Edwards

So fill the kettle, take a breath

Smile at your little nest

Let go of today's stress & sorrow

In the end, it can all wait til tomorrow

ONE DAY

We open our eyes

And that is the first victory

Feel each tiny cell

Every hair on our head

Wiggle our toes

Breathe in deep and clear

And slow

Allow the first breath to leave

And we say

One movement

One moment

One minute

And then the next

Because that is how we do this

One step at a time

Because nothing stays still forever

And one day we will be there

And not here

By taking these tiny steps

One at a time.

MOTHER

I hope you know

That the universe begins and ends

In you

That wild rivers flow inside your tiny heart

And ancient roots

and freshest buds

reach up from your little hands and down from your bare feet

into the warm earth

That every ocean exists behind your eyes

As deep as galaxies

Where stars are the gaps that your light breaks through

And every planet orbits you

And you are the moon in all her quiet,

humble charm

And the sun in all her dazzling glory

I hope you know that in you, the universe

begins and ends

And begins

Again

STILL

I can still see the haze
of the September sun through light mist
the cool yellow glow
low and soft
spread like butter across the horizon
blurring the lines

Distant clusters of friends
on their first walk back to school, charcoal against in the light
new shoes on wet leaves
fresh leather and flattened mulch
on the damp pavements

Little hands in big hands
some skipping with excitement
others with swirling tummies, nervous and sad

Memories of long, hot days
almost out of sight
beaches and bright colours now faded
into the burnt sienna and smooth grey
of early Autumn

The sense of discomfort
where all things new collide with the shedding of the Summer
and the taste of Winter to come

Laura Ding-Edwards

I can still smell the damp air
And hear the new winds rising

The harvest moon waits patiently for the sun to lose its power

And all is getting quieter

Still.

TOGETHER

It feels like life is not ok

And this "thing" will never go away

Like all around is caving in

And no-one knows where to begin

What-ifs and fears are on the rise

And nobody's able to disguise

The sadness of this sudden change

To life, routine; it's very strange

But sit a moment with that thought

Forget the things that you've been taught

For a while there's no rat race

A slower life put in its place

We suddenly have the space to stop

Appreciate the things we've got

The cusp of spring still breaks its sleep

Our birds return to trill & cheep

And hope & kindness start to bloom

As we find ways to lift the gloom

And so in this uncertain time

Take stock, reflect and redefine

Keep in mind it's not forever

We'll make it through with love, together

Authors Note; this particular poem was written during the COVID-19 pandemic, when everything stopped and for a few months during the start of 2020 the whole world seemed to slow right down. A very strange time & this poem barely scratches the surface of what was to come, but it was certainly my way of trying to make sense of the odd reality we found ourselves in.

Laura Ding-Edwards

LITTLE BOAT

A little boat in a great big sea
Feels so scary when it's just me
Bobbing along with no real course
Alone, no anchor, no help to source

No rest in storms, no common ground
No oars to row, or turn around
Just me, the boat and the great big sea
Nothing but space, but not feeling free

Absorbed in nothing all consuming
Threats of capsize ever looming
So focussed on the little boat
And all the ways to stay afloat

That in the distance, across the sea
I miss a voice that's calling me
A tiny speck a mile away
The voice gets closer, I hear it say

"You're not alone, I'm out here too
Bobbing along in this ocean blue
I've watched for days you float alone
And seen the ways in which you've grown"

Still

The boat approaches, steady, strong
Alongside mine before too long
And in this moment I can see
I wasn't stranded out at sea

Help was out there all along
I just tried too hard to be strong
And missed the other boats out there
The offers of a journey to share

So when you feel you're lost & grey
Know help is never far away
When you feel stranded, lost at sea
Just open your eyes & look for me

Laura Ding-Edwards

THE LONGEST MONTH

January; the longest month

A never-ending grey

Smothering and sorrowful

Night bleeds into day

Wind whipped and downtrodden

Sodden and soaked through

Knee deep mud & mucky boots

Miserable and blue

Silent mornings, deepest nights

No dawn trill to rouse

Stay warm in bed for longer

Than the snooze alarm allows

But February is on the move

Spring waits for her turn

A distant cuckoo, snowdrops

Then daffodils return

Hedgerows burst with fleshy green

Blossom births from rest

Crocus sprout in woodland

And fledglings fly the nest

For January will soon be done

As sure as Earth will spin

Appreciate this quiet time

Your Spring awaits within

WHAT IF

What if I'm not good enough?

I told her that the stars illuminating the heavy night don't worry whether the sky is dark enough

they just shine

What if I'm not brave enough?

I told her that the clear trickle of a mountain stream doesn't know it will become a crashing waterfall

it just flows

What if I'm not strong enough?

I told her the whispering wind can become a howling gale that can uproot the heaviest tree

What if I'm not beautiful enough?

I told her that those who only see beauty

on the outside have no sight on the inside

What if I'm not enough?

I told her

that when you are made to feel

you're not enough

it's often

that you are too much

TODAY

Today I thought about your birth, but then that's nothing new

I thought about it yesterday and will tomorrow too

A world awash with panic at a time with no solution

Fear and apprehension of a global mass pollution

Born into isolation, that's not how it's meant to be

You won't remember how things were, the year no-one was free

No precious newborn cuddles, no visitors allowed

No cosy chats with cups of tea, no welcome baby crowd

Gifts left on the doorstep, outdoor glances, far apart

So much tinier up close; My proud but aching heart

To you this life is normal, we speak only at a distance

And reaching out to touch a hand is met with sad resistance

You read the faces that you see, but only by their eyes

You don't know a life before this where we weren't all in disguise

Soon you'll learn to play in all the ways you can't yet know

So many firsts are waiting, just a little way to go

2020 did it's worst, you're the rose, it was the thorn

One day I'll tell you all about the year that you were born

ANOTHER LOVE

It was knowing that I loved you
But that was nor enough
It was knowing that you loved me too
Though love was raw and tough

It was almost something beautiful
So nearly something pure
But I knew what the answers were
And you were never sure

It was lightning, sparks and fireworks
A whirlwind, swept away
It was chaos, lust; a thunderstorm
And never meant to stay

It was midnight conversations
And rain on hot scorched earth
It was fire in our bellies
It was love, for what love's worth

It was secret, it was special
It was all I thought I knew
Of love and dreams and heroes
And all I had of you

It was fragile, made of glass
What I thought was stone was sand
And it slipped away before us
Like an ice cube in a hand

And all it left was water
Which gently drained away
Through the burnt and barren soil

Laura Ding-Edwards

What was left of our hey day

It was melancholy magic

It was all it was to be

It was us for just a moment

Now its just you, and me

It was something to remember

But something I left there

In the minutes and the memories

That we were bound to share

So let the sand slip downward

See the water soak away

Watch as the storm quietens

Another love, another day

I F

If Mama is a calming breeze
Then you're a calm breeze too
For everything that I possess
I've handed down to you

If Mama is a healing hand
Then you have these hands too
Use them wisely, little one
They have much work to do

If Mama is a goddess
You're the Queen of all the skies
Your heart is strong & mighty
And your soul is old & wise

If Mama is your home
Then that home is within you
Carry it around the world
But come back safely, too

If Mama is the Moon
Then you're the sprinkling of stars
The planets & the galaxies
Belong in us - they're ours

If Mama is the Earth
Then you're the vast & open sea

More powerful, mysterious

And much bigger than me

If Mama is the sands of time

Then you're infinity

You're everything and more

That I could ever hope to be

U N K N O W N

What happens to the love
That we never got to share
The moments that we missed
And the seconds that are spare

The flood of unspent feelings
That have nowhere to go
The whispers and the wonderlust
A heart that will not show

What happens to the parts of life
That didn't go quite right
The times we turned away
Followed dark instead of light

Do they exist among the stars
Or in the gaps between
The pieces of our broken souls
That nobody has seen

What happens to the versions
Of ourselves that we let die
The people we grew out of
And the ones who passed us by

Do our secrets die with memory
Or are they freed like birds

Laura Ding-Edwards

Once we return to earth & sky
With no more use for words

Do we become the universe
Or have we always been
The biggest part of everything
Unknown, unfound, unseen.

ADULTHOOD

Thank the stars

That we believed them

When they told us that growing up

Was something to look forward to

And rushed

Open arms

Open heart

Into the world

Thinking it was better than what we had

Constricted by time,

rules and uniforms

Bribery for bedtime

Mid afternoon clock off

And six weeks that felt like forever.

Imagine if we'd known

That childhood was the best

Most beautiful freedom

We would ever feel,

They'd have never convinced us

To leave it behind

So soon.

Prose

WORDS

Before you read the little quotes I have collaborated through this book, I want you to understand why these small phrases can be so important, whether they resonate with you or you pass them on to other people who might find them useful.

The two phrases that impacted me the most in my life are years apart and polar opposites;

"If as many people hated me as hate you I would kill myself"

"Someone is saving you for something special"

The first was said to me by a boy at school, two days before we left forever. I had been to three different high schools, a PRU and barely managed to have the confidence to go back to the school I originally started at. I was determined not to let bullies dictate my whole life forever and with the PRU only allowing me to take three GCSE's I battled back through mainstream school Year 11 just to get the grades I needed to scrape by. I managed to pass all 11 GCSEs, some Es a couple of A*s and everything in between. I think about that phrase often and remember how grateful I am that I didn't take his advice.

The second came after a car accident when I was 18. Driving back from my bar job I had a tyre blowout - my car rolled through concrete bollards, a street light and ploughed through a cemetery wall, eventually landing on all four wheels in the middle of the road. I don't remember getting out, my first memory is being about 200 yards away running barefoot up the road and looking back to see my bonnet on fire. I flagged a car down who called the emergency services. When the police arrived they asked how I had got out - I explained I had just opened the door and walked. He shone his torch and showed me the glass surrounding the car and told me that to have walked over that barefoot was impossible. He went on to say that he had seen cars with less damage that had been fatal and that clearly I had been saved for something special. Whenever I have felt down or useless, this sentence keeps me going.

Still

The point of this post isn't just to show how important the words we speak are, but to show you that other peoples opinions of you can be completely different.

Don't ever give more weight to one than the other; for every person who says something awful, there is someone else waiting to say something lovely.

GOOD VIBES

"Good Vibes Only" is a false and destructive narrative.

Embrace your bad days, allow yourself to feel sad, angry and disappointed. You are human. We only move through pain by acknowledging it exists.

PERFECT

It's not about being perfect, it's about making a decision to try and be better. It's about choosing to pull yourself up on unnecessary negativity towards others, it's about stopping for a second before you judge, its about giving the benefit of the doubt.

It's about deciding to change the language you use about yourself and other people.

It's never been about not making mistakes, it's about owning it when you do, reflecting on it and changing what you need in order to grow.

Remember that if you're not owning it you're passing it on.

R A W

You're going to love people who don't love you back, and that's going to be so hard, but please love yourself enough to never beg for their approval.

If people don't love you in all your raw, vulnerable beauty then don't change to suit them; you will understand in time why this is so much more important.

TOXIC POSITIVITY

You do not have to

Get over it

Man up

Keep calm and carry on

This is toxic positivity. Your sadness is valid, your lack of motivation is allowed. Your apathy is ok. You have permission to be unwell.

If you need to stop, cry, rest then do it.

We are only human and it would serve us to remember that.

REMINDER

When you go to bed this evening, remind yourself that you did the best you could with what you had today; tomorrow is a brand new day with a brand new energy.

CLOUDS

Choose the people who encourage the best version of you; the rest are just clouds passing through your blue sky.

Laura Ding-Edwards

STUPID

When people treat you like you're stupid, sometimes the best thing you can do is humour them.

MENTAL ILLNESS

Never have so many had so much to say on something they
know so little about.

ONE SMILE

You could be the reason someone chooses to keep fighting today.

One smile in the street, one kind word, one hug. One tiny ray of light in their darkness.

You are as essential to this world as the air we breathe – remember that.

F E A R

Every time you push past fear you prove your anxieties wrong, you show it up for the liar that it is and you take back your power.

I know how tough it is & I know how strong those feelings are, but the pay-off is so worth it.

It only takes one time, one journey, one step to start moving away from fear and into freedom.

DEEP

When you know how to stay afloat and trust in your own strength it doesn't matter how deep the water is.

ASSUMPTION

Just because someone has a newer car or a bigger house or a better paid job than you it doesn't mean they owe you anything. It doesn't mean you can direct your envy at them. It doesn't mean they are happy – suspend your assumptions.

HOPE

Hope survives where change is still necessary.

JOURNEY

When you feel you have miles to go it's the universe reminding you that you're not done yet.

Your journey isn't over – the best is yet to come.

Laura Ding-Edwards

RESPONSIBILITY

You are only responsible for your own actions and decisions, you cannot change anything other than yourself.

If you have made someone aware that their behaviour affects you negatively and there are no changes, the only thing that you are in charge of is how long that behaviour is ok for.

You can't force someone to care more about you, or treat you better, or love you harder. You absolutely cannot control somebody else's level of feeling – towards you, themselves, or anyone else.

If it's not enough, the only thing you can control is where your path goes next.

YOUR BEST

Your best is not a fixed level.

Sometimes your best is the top of your game, some days its just about surviving.

Your best is what you can do with what you have in that moment and that is always enough.

TRUTH

It's easier for some people to forgive a beautiful lie than the ugly truth; this will always feel uncomfortable if you are someone who values honesty, just be ready for it and stay in your truth, as tough as it is sometimes.

MESSY

We are existing on caffeine and shallow interactions and trying to keep up with the latest ideals of perfection, wondering why we feel so unfulfilled.

Allow yourself to go deeper; pick up bits of magic as you blindly follow your own path with no expectations and notice how much better it feels to discover your messy truth.

SAVIOUR

For an empath, one of the hardest things to accept is that you can't save everyone.

If you feel things deeply, someone shutting themselves down or not allowing you to be with them where they are can hit hard – it feels incredibly personal.

Please bear in mind that this is not a reflection on your love, your character or your heart.

People are allowed to choose their own method of growth, not everyone feels comfortable sharing their soul however good your intentions are. This is their journey, not yours and it is not your job to push them into your version of healing.

Accept that you cannot save everyone. Unless someone makes their healing your business, it is entirely theirs to hold and that is absolutely their right.

FAILURE

Don't underestimate the importance of the bits of your life that feel like failures at the time.

I quit my full time career at 18 because my anxiety just wouldn't allow me to do long periods of time 1:1 as a hairdresser. It was too intimate, too much pressure and too much responsibility. I got a job in a bar, which felt at the time like a step backwards, but I met some of my best friends there, I gained so much confidence and some amazing social skills and had the best two years of my life.

There are no failures – just changes. Everything you do has a purpose and a lesson, you just need to be able to change your perspective enough to find them.

STIGMA

You wouldn't feel ashamed or weak for taking a painkiller for a headache, so stop feeling ashamed or weak for needing medical help with a mental illness.

There is no difference. Both have a purpose, both are not within your control, both are necessary for some of us. You are part of the story of ending the stigma.

GUILTY

Can we please stop penalising illness as a society?

School, work, life – we are constantly praised for pushing beyond our limits and made to feel guilty if we say "enough". Sanctions and restrictions are put on us, attendance is incentivised, we are put on programmes and reports and have marks against our names for being human and we are drilled with the idea that our health is somehow a choice.

There is no single thing worse for morale than being made to feel we are less of a person because our health isn't 100% all of the time.

This is how people have breakdowns. This is how people literally work themselves so hard that their mind and body take the reins and force you to stop.

Take notice of the signs and try really hard to be the person that helps everyone to feel ok with being a normal human being, we all need to take a break before we actually break.

SELF LOVE

Loving yourself despite your flaws is incredible, but if you are refusing to analyse your behaviour too then you are stunting your own growth. There is always room to be kinder, gentler, less judgmental, more compassionate. The only way to practise true self love is to commit to always moving up, always learning, always trying to be a better person than you were yesterday.

LIGHT

We are conditioned to hide our success, to avoid compliments, to share our failures and shortcomings before our wins. We all fear judgement and jealousy.

You are entitled to celebrate your goodness and shine your light.

Nobody benefits if we all just sit in the dark.

Laura Ding-Edwards

MAGIC

The whole universe is waiting patiently for you to discover the magic that exists inside you.

YOUR PLACE

We live in a culture that leads us to believe that kindness is weakness, acceptance and tolerance is childish and forgiveness is wrong.

The loudest and most controversial voices attract the baying mob and this trend of intolerance, media witch hunts and grudges is the exact opposite of what the world needs to survive. Hate on hate, feeding off division and breeding more and more anger. Fearful people who survive by continually pointing out others' mistakes as if it's not an integral part of being human.

It's really important that we all remember that being on this side of the mob only protects us while we're in favour. Our stars can fall hard at any given moment, and it won't be the "snowflakes" that throw you under the bus.

Choose goodness and kindness, every time, even when it feels uncomfortable, even when it feels lonely. Choose your place wisely.

RISE

Have patience, darling.

The liars and cheats will out themselves to you eventually; you are water and they are stone. They exist only to sink to the bottom and help you rise.

ABOUT THE AUTHOR

Laura Ding-Edwards is a writer & artist from Herefordshire UK. She started her writing career in 2019, when the now world reknowned poem, The Mountain, was an instant hit on social media.

Alongside writing, Laura creates watercolour images to complement her poetry on prints and cards, which can be found on her website www.lauradingedwards.com.

Laura lives with her husband Ronnie and their daughter Dotty, who was born in 2020

RESOURCES AND SUPPORT

If you are struggling with your mental health or emotional wellbeing, please reach out to someone. The following UK organisations and resources all have mental health at the heart of their mission:-

THE FRANK BRUNO FOUNDATION

Aims to provide support, encouragement and the motivation to succeed for those experiencing or recovering from mental ill-health

www.thefrankbrunofoundation.co.uk

MIND

Empowers people to understand their condition and the choices available to them.

www.mind.org.uk

SAMARITANS

Free and confidential helpline and webchat open 24 hours a day, 365 days a year. Working together to make sure fewer people die by suicide.

www.samaritans.org

CALM (CAMPAIGN AGAINST LIVING MISERABLY)

Free and confidential helpline and webchat. Leading a movement against suicide.

www.thecalmzone.net

SASP [SUPPORT AFTER SUICIDE PROJECT]

Supporting those bereaved by suicide.

www.suportaftersuicide.org.uk

TIME TO CHANGE

Changing how we think and act about mental health problems.

www.time-to-change,org

YOUNG MINDS

Fighting for young people's mental health

www.youngminds.org.uk

Laura Ding-Edwards

ACKNOWLEDGEMENTS

First and foremost, my parents for always supporting me, gently encouraging my growth and always giving me a place to call home. You are my heroes and I will never be able to thank you enough for the lessons you have taught me about life.

My husband Ronnie for keeping my spirits up with his infectious optimism and my beautiful little girl Dotty for showing me the meaning of true love and giving me a reason to be grateful every single day.

My friends; my sanity who I will never stop being thankful for.

My publisher, Sean, for taking a chance on me with The Mountain and continuing to support me with Still.

My designer, Lynda, who has worked tirelessly to get this book looking so lovely.

And last, but definitely not least, everyone who has taken the time to read my work, whether online or by buying my work – thank you so much!